I0011572

Book 1
Cryptography
By Solis Tech

&

Book 2
CompTIA A+
By Solis Tech

Book 1
Cryptography
By Solis Tech

Cryptography Theory & Practice Made Easy!

Cryptography: Cryptography Theory & Practice Made Easy!

Table of Contents

Introduction..5

Chapter 1: Cryptography - History and Basic Concepts........................6

Chapter 2: The Modern Cryptography..9

Chapter 3: Cryptosystem - The Basics..10

Chapter 4: Different Types of Attacks on Cryptosystems....................16

Chapter 5: Traditional Cryptography..21

Chapter 6: Modern Cryptography Schemes...27

Chapter 7: The Pros and Cons of Cryptography.................................29

Conclusion...30

Introduction

I want to thank you and congratulate you for purchasing the book, *Cryptography*.

This book contains tips and techniques on how to build cryptosystems – even if you're just a complete beginner.

This eBook will help you learn about the history and basic principles of cryptography. It will teach you the different aspects of message encryption. In addition, you will learn how to establish cryptosystems. Aside from discussing modern/digital encryption schemes, this book will teach you how to use different types of "practical" ciphers.

Thanks again for purchasing this book. I hope you enjoy it!

Chapter 1: Cryptography – History and Basic Concepts

The Origin of Cryptography

During the ancient times, people needed to do two things: (1) to share information and (2) protect the information they are sharing. These things forced individuals to "encode" their messages. This "encoding" process protects the message in a way that only the intended recipient can understand the information. That means the data will remain secure even if unauthorized parties get access to it.

The art and science of protecting information is now known as "cryptography." The term "cryptography" was formed by fusing two Greek terms, "Krypto" (which means "hidden") and "graphene" (which means writing).

According to historians, cryptography and "normal" writing were born at the same time. As human civilizations progressed, people organized themselves into groups, clans, and kingdoms. These organizations led to the creation of concepts such as wars, powers, sovereignty, and politics. Obviously, these ideas involve information that cannot be shared with ordinary citizens. The group leaders needed to send and receive information through protected means. Thus, cryptography continued to evolve.

The Contributions of Egyptians and Romans

1. Egyptians

The oldest sample of cryptography can be found in Egypt. Ancient Egyptians used hieroglyphs (i.e. a system of writing that involves symbols and images) to share and record pieces of information. In general, these symbols and images are only intelligible to the priests who transmitted messages on behalf of the pharaohs. Here is a sample hieroglyph:

Fig. 1 - Egyptian Hieroglyphs

Several thousands of years later (around 600 to 500 BC), Egyptian scholars started to use simple substitution codes. This style of encoding involved the replacement and/or combination of two or more alphabets using a secret rule. This rule was considered as the "key" in retrieving the real message from the coded "garbage."

2. Romans

Ancient Romans used a system of cryptography known as the Caesar (or Shift) Cipher. This system depends on moving each letter of the message by a certain number (three is the most popular choice). To decode the information, the recipient simply needs to "move" the letters back using the same number. Here is an example:

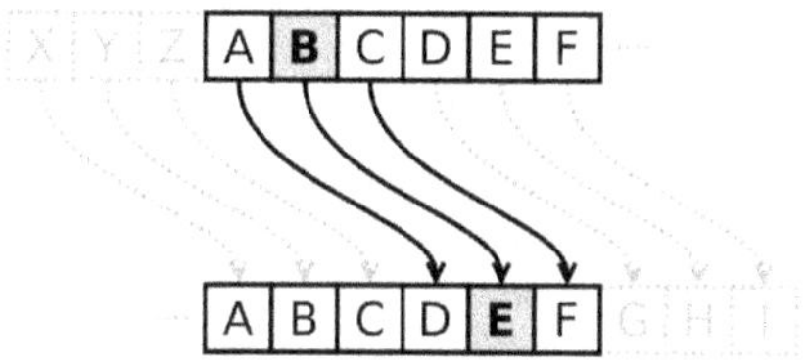

Fig. 2 – Caesar Cipher

Cryptography – Fundamental Concepts

Encryption – This is the process of converting information into an unintelligible form. It helps in securing the privacy of the message while it is being sent to the recipient.

Decryption – This process is the exact opposite of encryption. Here, the encoded message is returned to its natural form.

Important Note: Encryption and decryption requires specific rules in converting the data involved. These rules are known as the key. Sometimes, a single key is used to encrypt and decrypt information. However, there are certain scenarios where these two processes require different sets of keys.

Plaintext and Ciphertext – The term plaintext refers to data that can be read and used without the application of special techniques. Ciphertext, on the other hand, refers to data that cannot be read easily: the recipient needs to use certain decryption processes to get the "real" message.

Authentication – This is probably one of the most important aspects of cryptography. Basically, authentication serves as a proof that the information was sent by the party claimed in the encoded message.]

Let's illustrate this concept using a simple example: John sent a message to Jane. However, before replying, Jane wants to make sure that the message really came from John. This verification procedure can be conducted easily if John does "something" on the message that Jane knows only John can do (e.g. writing his signature, including a secret phrase, folding the letter in a certain way, etc.). Obviously, successful decryption of the message will be useless if the information came from an unwanted source.

Integrity – Loss of integrity is one of the biggest problems faced by people who use cryptography. Basically, loss of integrity occurs whenever the message gets altered while it is being sent to the receiver. Unnecessary and/or unwanted modifications in a message may cause misunderstanding and other issues. Because of this, the message must be protected while it is being delivered. Modern cryptographers accomplish this through the use of a cryptographic hash (i.e. a hash function that is extremely difficult to invert, modify, or recreate).

Non-Repudiation – This concept focuses on ensuring that the sender cannot deny that he/she sent the encoded message. In the example given above, it is important to make sure that John cannot deny the fact that he was the one who sent the message. Modern cryptography prevents this "sender repudiation" using digital signatures.

Chapter 2: The Modern Cryptography

For some people, modern cryptography is the foundation of technology and communications security. This type of cryptography is based on mathematical concepts like the number theory, the probability theory, and the computational-complexity theory. To help you understand modern cryptography, here is a comparison of the "classical" and "modern" types of cryptography.

Classical Cryptography

1. It utilizes common characters (e.g. letters and numbers) directly.
2. It relies heavily on the "obscure is secure" principle. The encryption and decryption processes were considered as confidential information. Only the people involved in the communication can access such data.
3. It needs an entire cryptosystem (will be explained in the next chapter) to complete the "confidential" transfer of information.

Modern Cryptography

1. It relies on modern technology like binary data sequences.
2. The information is encoded through the use of mathematical algorithms accessible to the public. Here, security is achieved through a "secret key" which is used as the foundation for the algorithms. Two factors ensure that "outsiders" cannot access the information even if they have the correct algorithm:
    a. It is extremely difficult to compute such algorithms. Thus, it is hard to extract any information from them.
    b. The absence or presence of secret keys.
3. The encryption doesn't involve the entire cryptosystem. Only the interested parties are required to participate in encoding and decoding the message.

Chapter 3: Cryptosystem – The Basics

A cryptosystem is the application of cryptographic methods and their appropriate coding environment (also called "infrastructure"). This system is used to add security to technology and communications services. Some people refer to cryptosystems as "cipher systems."

To illustrate the concept of cryptosystems, let's consider the following example:

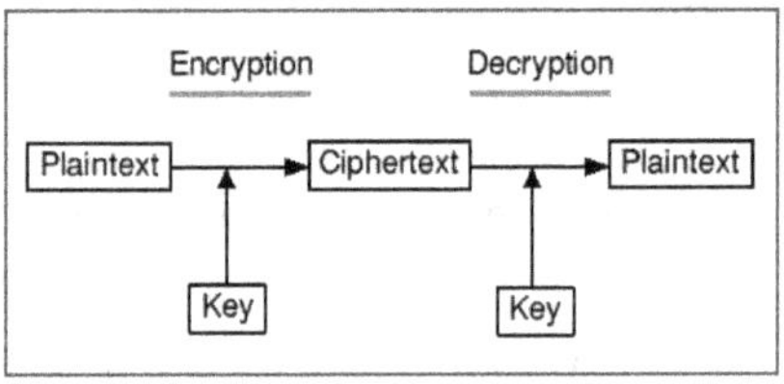

Fig. 3 – A Cryptosystem

In this example, the sender encrypts his message (i.e. the plaintext) through the use of a key. This process converts the plaintext into ciphertext. Once the receiver gets the ciphertext, he uses the same key to decrypt the information. Thus, the ciphertext will be turned into plaintext again.

As you can see, only the parties who have the "key" can access the shared information. Cryptosystems can be divided into these basic components:

- Plaintext – The information that needs to be shared and protected.
- Encryption Algorithm – The mathematical process that uses a plaintext and an encryption key to produce a ciphertext.
- Ciphertext – The coded version of the information. In general, cryptography protects the message itself, not the transmission. That means the coded message is sent through public channels such as emails. Thus, anyone who can access the selected delivery channel can intercept or compromise the message.
- Decryption Algorithm – It is a mathematical process that creates plaintext from any given set of ciphertext and decryption key. Basically, it reverses the encryption process done earlier in the transmission of the message.

- Encryption Key – The value provided by the sender. In creating the ciphertext, the sender enters this key (along with the plaintext) into the encryption algorithm.
- Decryption Key – The value known by the recipient. The decryption key is always related to the encryption key used for the message. However, these keys don't have to be identical. The recipient enters the decryption key and the ciphertext into the decryption algorithm in order to get the plaintext. The collection of all decryption keys for a cryptosystem is known as a "key space."

There are times when an interceptor (also called "attacker") tries to get the encoded message. In general, interceptors are unauthorized entities who want to access the ciphertext and determine the information it contains.

The Two Kinds of Cryptosystems

Currently, cryptosystems are divided into two kinds: (1) Symmetric Key Encryption and (2) Asymmetric Key Encryption. This way of classifying cryptosystems is based on the method of encryption/decryption used for the entire system.

The major difference between the symmetric and asymmetric encryptions is the connection between the encryption and decryption keys. Generally speaking, all cryptosystems involve keys that are closely related. It is impossible to create a decryption key that is totally unrelated to the code's encryption key. Let's discuss each kind of cryptosystems in more detail:

Symmetric Key Encryption

Cryptosystems that belong to this kind have a single key. This key is used to encrypt and decrypt the information being sent. The study of symmetric encryption and systems is known as "symmetric cryptography." Some people refer to symmetric cryptosystems as "secret key" systems. The most popular methods of symmetric key encryption are: IDEA, BLOWFISH, DES (Digital Encryption Standard), and 3DES (Triple-DES).

During the 1960s, 100% of the cryptosystems utilized symmetric encryption. This method of encrypting and decrypting information is so reliable and efficient that it is still being used even today. Businesses that specialize on Communications and Information Technology consider symmetric encryption as the best option available. Since this kind of encryption has distinct advantages over the asymmetric one, it will still be used in the future.

Here are the main characteristics of symmetrically encrypted cryptosystems:

- Before transmitting the message, the sender and the receiver must determine the key that will be used.
- The key must be changed regularly to avoid any intrusion into the cryptosystem.
- A stable form of data transmission must be established to facilitate easy sharing of the key between the involved parties. Since the keys must be changed on a regular basis, this mechanism may prove to be expensive and complicated.
- In an organization composed of "x" individuals, to facilitate two-way communication between any two members, the required number of keys for the entire system is derived using the formula: "x * (x-1)/2."
- The keys used are often small (i.e. measured through the number of bits involved), so the encryption and decryption processes are faster and simpler compared to those used for asymmetric systems.
- These cryptosystems do not require high processing capabilities from computer systems. Since the keys used are small and simple, ordinary computers can be used to establish and manage the cryptosystem.

Here are the two problems usually encountered when using this kind of cryptosystem:

- Key Determination – Before any message can be transmitted, the sender and the receiver must determine a specific symmetric key. That means a secure and consistent way of creating keys must be established.
- Trust Issues – Because all the people involved use the same key, symmetric key cryptography requires the sender to trust the receiver, and vice versa. For instance, if one of them shares the key with an unauthorized party, the security of the entire cryptosystem will be ruined.

Modern day communicators say that these two concerns are extremely challenging. Nowadays, people are required to exchange valuable data with non-trusted and non-familiar parties (e.g. seller and buyer relationships). Because of these problems, cryptographers had to develop a new encryption scheme: the asymmetric key encryption.

Asymmetric Key Encryption

These cryptosystems use different keys for encrypting and decrypting the message. Although the keys involved are dissimilar, they still have a logical and/or mathematical relationship. It is impossible to extract the message using a decryption key that is totally unrelated to the encryption key.

According to cryptographers, this mode of encryption was developed during the 20th century. It was developed in order to overcome the challenges related to symmetric key cryptosystems. The main characteristics of this encryption scheme are:

- Each member of the cryptosystem should have two different keys – a public key and a private key. When one of these keys is used for encryption, the other one must be used for decryption.
- The private key is considered as confidential information. Each member must protect the private key at all times. The public key, on the other hand, can be shared with anyone. Thus, public keys can be placed in a public repository. As such, some people refer to this scheme as "public key encryption."
- Although the private and public keys are mathematically related, it is practically impossible to determine a key using its "partner."
- When Member1 wants to send information to Member2, he needs to do three things:
    - Obtain Member2's public key from the public repository.
    - Encrypt the message.
    - Transmit the message to Member2. Member2 will acquire the original message using his private key.
- This mode of encryption involves larger and longer keys. That means its encryption and decryption processes are slower compared to those of symmetric encryption.
- The asymmetric key encryption requires high processing power from the computers used in the cryptosystem.

Symmetric key encryption is easy to comprehend. The asymmetric one, however, is quite difficult to understand.

You may be wondering as to how the encryption and decryption keys become related and yet prevent intruders from acquiring a key using its "partner." The answer to this question lies in mathematical principles. Today, cryptographers can create encryption keys based on these principles. Actually, the concept of asymmetric key cryptography is new: system intruders are not yet familiar with how this encryption works.

Here is the main problem associated with asymmetric key cryptosystems:

- Each member needs to trust the cryptosystem. He/she has to believe that the public key used for the transmission is the correct one. That person must convince himself that the keys in the public repository are safe from system intruders.

  To secure the cryptosystem, companies often use a PKI (Public Key Infrastructure) that involves a reputable third party organization. This "outside organization" manages and proves the authenticity of the keys used in the system. The third party company has to protect the public keys and provide the correct ones to authorized cryptosystem members.

Because of the pros and cons of both encryption methods, business organizations combine them to create safer and practical security systems. Most of these businesses are in the communications and information technology industries.

Kerckhoff's Principle

During the 19th century, a Dutch cryptographer named Auguste Kerckhoff identified the requirements of a reliable cryptosystem. He stated that a cryptosystem must be secure even if everything related to it – except the keys – are available to the public. In addition, Mr. Kerckhoff established six principles in designing new cryptosystems. These principles are:

1. The cryptosystem needs to be unbreakable (i.e. in a practical sense). This excludes the system's vulnerability to mathematical intrusions.

2. The system should be secure enough that members can still use it even during an attack from unauthorized entities. The cryptosystem needs to allow authorized members to do what they need to do.

3. The keys used in the system must be easy to change, memorize, and communicate.

4. The resulting ciphertexts must be transmissible by unsecure channels such as telegraph.

5. The documents and devices used in the encryption system must be portable and easy to operate.
6. Lastly, the system must be user-friendly. It should not require high IQ or advanced memorization skills.

Modern cryptographers refer to the second rule as the Kerckhoff principle. They apply it in almost all encryption algorithms (e.g. AES, DES, etc.). Experts in this field consider these algorithms to be completely secure. In addition, these experts believe that the security of the transmitted message relies exclusively on the protection given to the private encryption keys used.

Maintaining the confidentiality of the encryption and decryption algorithms may prove to be a difficult problem. Actually, you can only keep these algorithms secret if you will share them with a few individuals.

Today, cryptography must meet the needs of internet users. Since more and more people gain access to hacking information and advanced computers, keeping an algorithm secret is extremely difficult. That means you should always use the principles given by Kerckhoff in designing your own cryptosystems.

Chapter 4: Different Types of Attacks on Cryptosystems

Nowadays, almost every aspect of human life is affected by information. Thus, it is necessary to safeguard important data from the intrusions of unauthorized parties. These intrusions (also called attacks) are usually classified based on the things done by the intruder. Currently, attacks are classified into two types: passive attacks and active attacks.

Passive Attacks

Passive attacks are designed to establish unauthorized access to certain pieces of information. For instance, activities such as data interception and tapping on a communication channel are considered as passive attacks.

These activities are inherently passive: they do not attempt to modify the message or destroy the channel of communication. They simply want to "steal" (i.e. see) the information being transmitted. Compared to stealing physical items, stealing data allows the legitimate owner (i.e. the receiver) to possess the information after the attack. It is important to note that passive data attacks are more harmful than stealing of physical items, since data theft may be unnoticed by the receiver.

Active Attacks

Active attacks are meant to alter or eliminate the information being sent. Here are some examples:

- Unauthorized modification of the message.
- Triggering unauthorized transmission of data.
- Modification of the data used for authentication purposes (e.g. timestamp, sender's information, etc.).
- Unauthorized removal of information.
- Preventing authorized people from accessing the information. This is known as "denial of service."

Modern cryptography arms people with the tools and methods for preventing the attacks explained above.

The Assumptions of a Cryptosystem Attacker

This section of the book will discuss two important things about system attacks: (1) cryptosystem environments and (2) the attacks used by unauthorized parties to infiltrate cryptosystems.

The Cryptosystem Environment

Before discussing the types of data attacks, it is important to understand the environment of cryptosystems. The intruder's knowledge and assumptions about this factor greatly influence his choices of possible attacks.

In the field of cryptography, three assumptions are made about the attacker and the cryptosystem itself. These assumptions are:

1. Information about the Encryption Method – Cryptosystem developers base their projects on two kinds of algorithms:

    i. Public Algorithms – These algorithms share information with the public.

    ii. Proprietary Algorithms – These algorithms keep the details of the cryptosystem within the organization. Only the users and designers can access information about the algorithm.

    When using a proprietary (or private) algorithm, cryptographers obtain security through obscurity. In general, these are developed by people within the organization and are not thoroughly checked for weaknesses. Thus, private algorithms may have loopholes that intruders can exploit.

    In addition, private algorithms limit the number of people that can join the system. You can't use them for modern communication. You should also remember Kerckoff's principle: "The encryption and decryption keys hold the security of the entire cryptosystem. The algorithms involved can be shared with the public."

    Thus, the first assumption is: "The attacker knows the encryption and decryption algorithms."

2. Obtainability of the Ciphertext – The ciphertext (i.e. the encrypted information) is transmitted through unsecured public channels. Because of this the second assumption is: "The attacker can access ciphertexts created by the cryptosystem."

3. Obtainability of the Ciphertext and the Plaintext – This assumption is more obscure than the previous one. In some situations, the attacker may obtain both the plaintext and the ciphertext. Here are some sample scenarios:

i. The attacker convinces the sender to encrypt certain pieces of information and gets the resulting ciphertext.

ii. The recipient may share the decrypted information with the attacker. The attacker obtains the corresponding ciphertext from the communication channel used.

iii. The attacker may create pairs of plaintexts and ciphertexts using the encryption key. Since the encryption key is in the public domain, potential attackers can access it easily. It's a "hit and miss" type of tactic.

Cryptographic Attacks

Obviously, every attacker wants to break into the cryptosystem and obtain the plaintext. To fulfill this objective, the attacker simply needs to identify the decryption key. Obtaining the algorithms is easy since the information is available publicly.

This means the attacker focuses on obtaining the secret decryption key. Once he/she gets this information, the cryptosystem is broken (or compromised).

Cryptographic attacks are divided into several categories. These are:

- BFA (Brute Force Attack) – Here, the intruder tries to find the decryption key by entering all possible information. For instance, the key contains 8 bits. That means the total number of possible keys is 256 (i.e. 2^8). The attacker tries all of these keys in order to obtain the plaintext. The longer the key, the longer the time needed for successful decryption.

- COA (Ciphertext Only Attack) – This tactic requires the complete set of ciphertexts used for a message. When COA gets the plaintext from the given ciphertexts, the tactic is considered successful. Attackers may also get the corresponding encryption key using this attack.

- CPA (Chosen Plaintext Attack) – This attack requires the attacker to work on the plaintext he/she selected for encryption. Simply put, the attacker has the plaintext-ciphertext combination. It means the task of decrypting the information is easy and simple. It is the first part of the attack – convincing the sender to encrypt certain pieces of information – that presents the most difficulties.

- KPA (Known Plaintext Attack) – With this tactic, the attacker should know some parts of the plaintext. He/she has to use this knowledge to obtain the rest of the message.
- Birthday Attack – This is a subtype of the brute force approach. Attackers use this tactic when working against cryptographic hash functions. Once the intruder finds two inputs that produce similar values, a collision is said to occur: the hash function is broken and the system is breached.
- MIM Attack (Man in the Middle Attack) – This attack is particularly designed for public key cryptosystems. In general, these systems require the exchange of keys before the actual transmission of the ciphertext. Here is an example:
    - Member1 wants to send a message to Member2. To do this, he sends a request for Member2's public key.
    - An intruder blocks the request and sends his own public key.
    - Thus, the unauthorized party acquires the information that will be sent by Member1.
    - To avoid detection, the intruder encrypts the data again and sends it to Member2.
    - The intruder uses his own public key. That means Member2 will see the attacker's key instead of Member1's.
- SCA (Side Channel Attack) – This attack is used to exploit the weaknesses of a cryptosystem's physical implementation. Here, the attackers ignore the system's algorithms and digital protection.
- Fault Analysis Attacks – When using this attack, the intruder looks for errors produced by the system. He/she uses the resulting information to breach the system's defenses.
- Timing Attacks – Here, attackers use the fact that different calculations require different processing times. These people can acquire some data about the message processed by a computer system. They do this by measuring the time used by the computer in performing its calculations.
- Power Analysis Attacks – These attacks are similar to the previous one. However, instead of time, they use the amount of power consumed by the

computer system. This information is used to determine the nature of the plaintext.

An Important Note About Cryptographic Attacks

The attacks explained above are theoretical and highly academic. Actually, most of those attacks are defined by cryptography instructors. Some of the attacks you read about involve unrealistic assumptions about the attacker and/or the system's environment.

However, these attacks have excellent potential. Attackers may find ways to improve them. It would be great if you will still consider these attacks when designing your own cryptosystems.

Chapter 5: Traditional Cryptography

You have learned about the basics of modern cryptography. You also discovered the different tools that you can use in designing your own cryptosystems. One of the powerful tools at your disposal is the symmetric key encryption: a mode of encryption that uses a single key for the entire communication process.

This chapter will discuss this mode further so you will know how to apply it in developing cryptosystems.

Old Cryptographic Systems

At this point, you have to study the cryptosystems used in the ancient times. These "old systems" share similar characteristics, which are:

- These cryptosystems are based on the symmetric mode of encryption.
- The message is protected using a single tool: confidentiality.
- These systems use alphabets to facilitate encryption. In contrast, modern cryptosystems use digital data and binary numbers to encrypt a message.

These old systems are called "ciphers." Basically, a cipher is just a group of procedures performed in order to encrypt and decrypt data. You may think of these procedures as the "algorithms" of these ancient cryptosystems.

1. The Caesar Cipher

This cipher is based on a single alphabet. Here, you can create a ciphertext just by replacing every letter of the message with a different one. Cryptologists consider this cipher as the simplest scheme today.

The Caesar Cipher is also called "shift cipher," since each letter is shifted by a fixed number. If you are using the English alphabet, you can use the numbers from 0 to 25. The people involved must choose a certain "shift number" before encoding the plaintext. The number will serve as the encryption and decryption key for the entire communication process.

How to Use the Shift Cipher

1. The sender and the receiver select a shift number.
2. The sender writes down the alphabet twice (i.e. a-z followed by a-z).
3. That person gets the plaintext and finds the appropriate letters. However, he moves the letters based on the shift number selected. For example, if

they are using the number 1, he will replace the letter "A"s with "B"s, the "B"s with "C"s, and so on.

4. The encryption procedure is done once all of the letters have been shifted.
5. The sender transmits the ciphertext to the receiver.
6. The receiver moves the letters of the ciphertext backwards, depending on the shift number being used.
7. Once all of the letters have been shifted, the decryption process is completed. The receiver can use the information he received from the sender.

The Cipher's Security Value

This is not a secure system since the possible encryption keys are extremely limited. If you are using the English alphabet, your possible keys are restricted to 25. This number is not enough for those who need more security. In this situation, an attacker may acquire your key just by carrying out a thorough key search.

2. The Simple Substitution Cipher

This is an improved version of the Caesar Cipher. Instead of using numbers to determine the ciphertext, you will choose your own equivalent for each letter of the alphabet. For instance, "A.C... X.Z" and "Z.X... C.A" are two simple permutations of the letters in the English alphabet.

Since this alphabet has 26 letters, the total permutations can be derived through this formula: $4x10^{26}$. The people involved can select any of these permutations to create the ciphertext. The permutation scheme serves as the key for this cryptosystem.

How to Use this Cipher

1. Write down the letters from A to Z.
2. The involved parties choose a permutation for each letter. For example, they might replace the "A"s with "F"s, the "B" with "W", etc. These new letters don't need to have any logical or mathematical relationship with the letter they represent.

3. The sender encrypts the plaintext using the selected permutations.
4. The message is sent to the receiver.
5. The receiver decodes the ciphertext using the chosen permutations.

The Cipher's Security Value

This cipher is way much stronger than the Caesar Cipher. Even strong computer systems cannot decode the ciphertext since the possible permutations (i.e. 4×10^{26}) are too many. Cryptosystems based on this cipher can stop attackers that rely on a brute force approach. However, this substitution system is based on a simple scheme. In fact, attackers have succeeded in breaking letter permutations in the past.

The Monoalphabetic and Polyalphabetic Ciphers

Monoalphabetic Ciphers are ciphers that rely on a single encryption system. In other words, a single encryption alphabet is used for each "normal" alphabet throughout the entire communication process. For instance, if "C" is encoded as "X", "C" must be written as "X" each time it appears in the plaintext.

The two encryption systems discussed above belong to this type.

Polyalphabetic Ciphers, on the other hand, involve multiple encryption alphabets. The encryption alphabets may be switched at different segments of the encryption procedure. Here are two examples of polyalphabetic ciphers:

The Playfair Cipher

This encryption scheme uses pairs of letters to create encryption alphabets. Here, the people involved must create a table where letters are written down. The table used is a 5x5 square (i.e. 25 in total): the squares inside the table hold the letters of the alphabet. Since there are 26 letters in the English alphabet, a letter must be omitted. Cryptographers often omit the letter "J" when using this cipher.

The sender and the receiver must choose a certain keyword, say "lessons." They must write this keyword in the key table, from left to right. In addition, they should not repeat letters. Once the word is written down, the sender/receiver must complete the table using the unused letters (i.e. alphabetically arranged). With the word "lessons" as the keyword and J omitted, the key table should look like this:

L	E	S	O	N
A	B	C	D	F
G	H	I	K	M
P	Q	R	T	U
V	W	X	Y	Z

How to Use this Cipher

1. You should split the message into diagraphs (i.e. pairs of letters). If the total number of letters is an odd number, you should add a Z to the last letter. As an example, let's encrypt the word "human" using the key table created above. It will look like this:

   HU MA NZ

2. Here are the encryption rules:

   a. If both letters are in the same column, you should use the letter under each one. You have to go back to the top if you are using the bottom letter. In our example, N and Z are in the same column. Thus, this pair becomes FN.

   b. If both letters are placed in the same row, use the letter located at the right of each one. You need to go back to the first letter of the row if you are working on the rightmost letter. (This rule doesn't apply to our example.)

   c. If none of the previous rules apply, create a rectangle using the pair of letters. Afterward, use the letters on the opposite corner of the correct letters. Work on the letters horizontally. According to this rule, the HU pair is converted to MQ (look at the key table). MA, on the other hand, becomes GF.

3. Using these rules, the word "human" becomes MQ GF FN when encrypted using the Playfair Cipher.

4. You just have to reverse the process if you want to decrypt the message.

The Playfair Cipher's Security Value

This scheme is stronger than the systems discussed earlier. Attackers will have a difficult time analyzing all of the possible keys. In general, cryptologists use this cipher to protect important information. Lots of people rely on the Playfair Cipher since it is easy to use and doesn't require special tools.

The Vigenere Cipher

This encryption scheme uses a word (also known as text string) as the key. This key is used to change the plaintext. For instance, let's use the word "human" as the key. You should convert each letter into its numeric value (i.e. A = 1, B = 2, etc.). In our example:

H = 8, U = 21, M = 13, A = 1, N = 14

How to Use this Cipher

1. If you want to encrypt "cold water," you have to write the letters down. Then, write the key numbers (i.e. 8, 21, 13, 1, and 14) under the words, one number for each letter. Repeat the numbers as necessary. It looks like this:

C	O	L	D	W	A	T	E	R
8	21	`13	1	14	8	21	13	1

2. Shift the letters of the normal alphabet according to the number written on the table. Here it is:

C	O	L	D	W	A	T	E	R
8	21	13	1	14	8	21	13	1
K	J	Y	E	K	I	O	R	S

3. As you can see, each letter of the plaintext is moved by a different amount – the amount is specified by the key. The letters of your key should be less than or equal to that of your message.

4. To decrypt the message, you just have to use the same key and shift the letters backward.

The Vigenere Cipher's Security Value

This cipher offers excellent security: better than the three ciphers discussed above. Cryptographers use this encryption system to protect military and political data. Because of its apparent invulnerability, security experts call this the "unbreakable cipher."

Chapter 6: Modern Cryptography Schemes

Nowadays, cryptographers use digital data to establish encryption systems. This data is often represented as sets of binary digits (also called "bits"). Modern cryptosystems must process these binary strings to create more strings. Symmetric encryption techniques are categorized based on the procedures performed on the digital information. These categories are:

Block Ciphers

These ciphers group the digital data into separate blocks and process them one at a time. The number of bits contained in a data block is predetermined and unchangeable. Two popular block ciphers, AES and DES, have block sizes of 128 and 64, respectively.

In general, a block cipher uses a set of plaintext data and produces a set of ciphertext data, usually of the same size. Once the block size is assigned, it can no longer be modified. The block size used for the system doesn't affect the strength of encryption techniques involved. The strength of this cipher relies on the length of its key.

Block Size

Although you can use any block size, there are some things you have to consider when working on this aspect of your cryptosystem. These are:

- Avoid small block sizes – Let's assume that a block size is equal to m. Here, the total number of possible plaintext combinations is 2^m. If an intruder acquires the plaintext data used for previous messages, he/she can initiate a "dictionary attack" against your cryptosystem. Dictionary attacks are performed by creating a dictionary of ciphertext and plaintext pairs generated using an encryption key. You should remember this simple rule: the smaller the block size, the weaker the system is against dictionary attacks.

- Don't use extremely large block sizes – Large block sizes mean more processing time for your computer system. Cryptographers working on large bit sizes experience efficiency issues. Often, the plaintext must be padded in order to get the desired block size.

- Use a block size that is a multiple of 8 – Computers can easily handle binary digits that are multiples of 8. You can take advantage of this fact by choosing a block size that has this mathematical property.

Different Types of Block Cipher Schemes

Cryptographers use a variety of block cipher encryption schemes in their systems. Here are some of the most popular block ciphers being used today:

- AES (Advanced Encryption Standard) – This cipher is based on Rijndael, an award-winning encryption algorithm.
- IDEA – This is considered as one of the strongest ciphers available. Its block size is equal to 64 while its key size is equal to 128 bits. Many applications utilize this encryption. For instance, the old versions of PGP (Pretty Good Privacy) protocol used IDEA extensively. Because of patent issues, the utilization of this encryption scheme is restricted.
- DES (Digital Encryption Standard) – This is the most popular block cipher during the 1990s. Because of their small size, DES ciphers are now considered as "broken ciphers."

Stream Ciphers

With this scheme, the information is encrypted one binary digit at a time. The resulting ciphertext is equivalent to the data processed (e.g. 10 bits of plaintext produce 10 bits of ciphertext). Basically, stream ciphers are block ciphers with a block size limit of 1 bit.

Chapter 7: The Pros and Cons of Cryptography

This chapter will discuss the pros and cons of using cryptography.

The Pros

Today, security experts consider cryptography as one of their most useful tools. It provides four things needed for modern communication:

1. Authentication – Cryptographic techniques like digital signatures prevent spoofing and data forgeries.

2. Confidentiality – Encryption schemes protect information from unauthorized parties.

3. Non-repudiation – The digital signatures used in cryptography prove the identity of the sender. Thus, disputes regarding this factor are prevented.

4. Data Integrity – Cryptography involves hash functions that can maintain the integrity of the data being transmitted.

The Cons

Nothing is perfect. Here are the problems associated with cryptography:

- Legitimate users may encounter issues when accessing well-encrypted information. This can turn into a disaster if a certain piece of information has to be obtained quickly.

- Constant availability of information – a basic aspect of communications and information technology – is hard to secure when using cryptography.

- Cryptosystems prevent selective access control. Some organizations need to provide exclusive file access to certain officers. When using cryptosystems, these organizations will have problems in giving selective access to their chosen members. This is because cryptosystems apply the same security measures on every file.

Conclusion

Thank you again for purchasing this book!

I hope this book was able to help you master the basics of cryptography.

The next step is to build your personal cryptosystems so you can easily encrypt messages.

Finally, if you enjoyed this book, please take the time to share your thoughts and post a review on Amazon. It'd be greatly appreciated!

Thank you and good luck!

Book 2
CompTIA A+
By Solis Tech

All-in-One Certification Exam Guide for Beginners!

Table Of Contents

Introduction..**34**

Chapter 1: The CompTIA A+ Examination..**35**

Chapter 2: The Different Parts of a Computer....................................**37**

Chapter 3: How to Work With Computer Parts Effectively................**44**

Chapter 4: The Tools Needed for Checking Computer Parts.............**48**

Chapter 5: Operating Systems..**51**

Conclusion...**54**

Introduction

I want to thank you and congratulate you for purchasing the book, *"CompTIA A+: All-in-One Certification Exam Guide for Beginners!"*

This book contains proven steps and strategies on how to prepare for the CompTIA A+ exams.

This eBook will explain the basics of the CompTIA A+ certification and tests. It will also give you some pointers regarding the topics that you need to review. By reading this book, you will gain the knowledge and skills required to pass the tests.

Thanks again for purchasing this book, I hope you enjoy it!

Chapter 1: The CompTIA A+ Examination

This eBook is written for people who are knowledgeable about computers. It assumes that you know to how to use a computer and its peripherals (e.g. printers, modems, etc.). This book will serve as your guide in preparing for the CompTIA A+ exam.

The A+ Certification

This is a certification program developed by CompTIA (Computer Technology Industry Association). This program is designed to provide a consistent way of checking the competency of computer technicians. The A+ certificate is given to people who have reached the degree of knowledge and diagnostic skills required to give proper support in the PC industry.

The A+ certification is similar to other programs in the industry (e.g. Microsoft Certified Systems Engineer and Novell's Certified Novel Engineer). The principle behind these certification programs is that if you need to get services for their products, you want to find technicians who have been certified by these programs.

The Benefits of Being A+ Certified

There are many reasons to get your own A+ certification. The information packet distributed by CompTIA gives the following benefits:

- It serves as a proof of your professional achievement.
- It improves your marketability.
- It gives you excellent advancement opportunities.
- It is now considered as a requirement for other kinds of advanced computer training.
- It encourages customers to do business with you

How to Become Certified

The A+ certification is given to anyone who passes the exams. You are not required to work for any company. CompTIA is not a secret group or society. It is, on the other hand, a group of elite computer technicians. If you want to be A+ certified, you have to do these things:

- Pass the exam called A+ Essentials
- Pass one of the three technician examinations:

- IT Technician Test
- Depot Technician Test
- Remote Support Technician Test

You can take the tests at any Pearson VUE or Thompson Prometric testing center. If you will pass both exams, you will receive a mail from CompTIA. That letter will inform you that you passed the tests. Additionally, it contains the certificate, a lapel pin, and a business card.

How to Sign Up for the Exams

To sign up for the tests, you may call Pearson VUE at 1-877-551-7587 or register online at www.vue.com. For Thompson Prometric, call 1-800-777-4276 or visit the website www.2test.com.

These companies will ask for your name, employer, phone number, mailing address, and SSN (Social Security Number). If you don't want to give out your SSN, a provisional number will be given to you. Additionally, they will ask when and where you want to take the exam.

Obviously, the exams aren't free. You have to pay your chosen testing company. That means you have to specify the payment arrangement during the registration process. You can simply provide your credit card information to the customer representative you will talk to. If you're doing it online, you can enter the credit card info on their payment page.

Who Should Use This Book?

If you want to pass the A+ tests, and do it confidently, you should use this book as a guide for your preparations. The A+ Essentials test is created to measure basic skills for an entry-level computer technician. The technician tests are designed to certify that you have the required skills to service microcomputer hardware.

This eBook was created with one purpose in mind: to help you pass the A+ exams. This guide will do that by explaining the things on which you will be tested.

Chapter 2: The Different Parts of a Computer

A PC (i.e. personal computer) is a machine made up of different components that work together to perform tasks (e.g. helping you write a document or add up large numbers). With this definition, notice that computers are described as having various distinct parts that work together harmoniously. Nowadays, almost all computers are modular. That is, they possess parts that can be replaced if the owner wants to improve the performance of his device. Each part has a specific purpose. In this chapter, you'll learn about the parts that make up a common PC, how they work, and what their functions are.

Important Note: Unless stated otherwise, the terms "computer" and "PC" can be used interchangeably throughout this eBook.

The Different Parts of a Motherboard

The motherboard, also called the system or planar board, serves as the "spine" of a PC. This is the brown or green circuit board that you'll find at the bottom of your computer. The system board is the most important part of a PC since it houses and/or connects the other parts of a computer together.

Different Types of Motherboards

There are two main types of motherboards. These are:

Integrated Motherboards – With this type, most of the parts are integrated into the system board's circuitry. Basically, integrated motherboards are created for simplicity. Since majority of the components are already part of the board itself, you won't have to install them individually. However, this simplicity has a major drawback: once a component stops working, you cannot simply replace it; you have to replace the entire motherboard. These boards are cheap to manufacture but expensive to repair.

Note: If one of the parts breaks, you may just disable it and add an expansion card that has similar capabilities.

Nonintegrated Motherboards – Here, the major parts (e.g. disk controllers, video circuitry, etc.) are installed as expansion cards. You will easily identify this kind of system board since every expansion slot is occupied by a major component.

The Different Form Factors of Motherboards

Computer experts also classify motherboards according to their design (also known as *form factor*). Here are the main form factors being used today: NLX, BTX, ATX, and micro ATX. You have to be vigilant when buying a computer case and system board separately. Some cases lack flexibility: they might not accommodate the system board you will select.

Let's discuss each form factor:

1. NLX – This is the abbreviation for "New Low-profile Extended". In general, this form factor is used for cases that are low-profile. With this design, the expansion slots (e.g. PCI, ISA, etc.) are placed on a special card to reduce the vertical space they occupy. Daughter boards, or adapter cards, that are normally plugged vertically into the expansion slots, are placed parallel to the system board. That means their size won't affect that of the computer case.

2. BTX – This form factor was launched by Intel back in 2003. With this design, the head-producing parts are lined up against the power supply's exhaust fan and the air intake vents. Then, the other components are cooled by installing heat sinks on the motherboard. This design offers a quiet setup since it involves efficient airflow paths and fewer exhaust fans.

3. ATX – With ATX motherboards, the processor and memory slots form a 90° angle with the expansion cards. This design places the memory and processor in line with the power supply's exhaust fan. Thus, the processor can remain cool while it runs. In addition, you may add expansion cards (even the full-length ones) to an ATX motherboard since the memory and processor are not parallel to the expansion cards.

4. Micro ATX – This form factor is similar with the previous one, with one major difference: it is designed for smaller computer cases. Micro ATX motherboards benefit from the enhanced cooling designs of their full-sized counterparts. However, since they are smaller, they have lesser motherboard headers, integrated components, expansion slots, and memory modules.

Processors – Their Functions and Characteristics

Now that you are familiar with system boards, you have to learn about their most important part: the central processing unit (CPU). The CPU controls all of the computer's activities using both internal and external buses. Basically, it is a processor chip that contains millions of transistors.

Important Note: Nowadays, the word "chip" describes the whole package that a computer technician may install into a socket. However, this word was originally used to refer to the silicon wafer hidden inside the carrier (i.e. the "chip" you see on your motherboard). The pins that you see on the outer part of the carrier are connected to the silicon wafer's small contacts. These pins allow you to install the carrier into a socket.

You can identify which part inside the PC is the central processing unit: the CPU is a large square that lies flat on the motherboard with a large fan and heat sink.

The Features of Modern Processors

- Hyperthreading – This word refers to HTT (hyper-threading technology). Basically, HTT is a variant of SMT (simultaneous multithreading). This kind of technology uses the scalar architecture of modern CPUs.

  HTT-capable CPUs appear as two different processors to the computer's operating system (OS). Because of this, the OS may assign two processes simultaneously, such as symmetric multi-processing, where multiple processors utilize the same network resources. Actually, the OS should support SMP in order to use HTT. If a process fails because of missing information caused by, for instance, branch prediction problems, the processor's execution resources can be reassigned for a different procedure that can be conducted immediately. Thus, the processor's downtime is dramatically reduced.

- Multicore – A CPU that has a multicore design contains two processors inside the same package. Here, the OS may treat the CPU as if it were two different CPUs. Just like the HTT, the OS should support SMP. Additionally, SMP is not considered as an upgrade if the apps run on the SMP system are not meant for parallel processes. A good example for the multicore technology is the i7 Quad-Core Processor from Intel.

- Microcode – This is the group of instructions (also called instruction set) that compose the different microprograms that the CPU executes as it performs its functions. The MMX (multimedia extensions) is a special example of an individual microprogram that performs a specific instruction set. Basically, microcodes are at a lower level than the codes used in computer programs. On average, each instruction from a computer program requires a large number of microinstructions. Intel and other processor manufacturers incorporate the MMX instruction set into their products.

- Overclocking – This feature allows you to increase the performance of your CPU, on par with processors created to function at overclocked rates. However, unlike processors created to function on that speed, you have to make sure that the overclocked processor doesn't damage itself from the increased level of heat. You might need to install an advanced cooling system (e.g. liquid cooling) to protect the CPU and other computer parts.

- Throttling – Processor throttling, also called clamping, is the process that specifies the CPU time to be spent on a computer program. By specifying how individual programs use the processor, you can "treat" all of the applications fairly. The principle of Application Fairness turns into a major problem for servers, where each program may represent the work of another user. That means fairness to computer programs becomes fairness to the users (i.e. the actual customers). Customers of modern terminal servers take advantage of this feature.

Memory – Its Functions and Characteristics

Nowadays, memory is one of the easy, popular, and inexpensive methods to enhance a computer. While the computer's processor runs, it stores data in the machine's memory. Basically, the more memory a machine has, the faster it can operate.

To determine the memory of a computer, search for thin sets of small circuit boards that are packed together near the CPU. These circuit boards sit vertically on the computer's motherboard.

How to Check for Errors in a Computer's Memory

Parity Checking

This is a basic scheme used to check for errors. It lines up the computer chips in a single column and separates them into equal bit groups. These bits are numbered beginning at zero. All of the number *x* bits, one from every chip, create a numerical array. If you are using "even parity", for instance, you will count up the number of bits contained in the array. If the total number is even, you will set the parity bit to zero since the bit count is already even. If the total is an odd number, on the other hand, you should set the parity bit to 1 in order to even up the bit count.

This technique is effective in identifying the existence of errors in the arrays of bits. However, it cannot indicate the location of the errors and how to solve them. Keep in mind that this isn't error correction – it is just a simple error check.

ECC

ECC stands for *Error Checking and Correcting*. If the computer's memory supports this method, the system will generate and store check bits. Whenever the machine accesses its memory, an algorithm will be performed on the check bits. If the result turns out to be zero (or a group of zeros), the information contained in the memory is considered valid and the computer functions as normal. ECC can identify single-bit and double-bit errors. However, it can only correct errors that are single-bit in nature.

The Four Main Types of Memory

- DRAM – This is perhaps the most popular type of RAM out there. DRAM stands for *Dynamic Random Access Memory*. Because of their inherent simplicity, these memory chips are cheap and easy to create compared to the other types. This kind of memory is called dynamic since it needs constant update signals in order to keep storing the data written there. If the DRAM chips won't receive stable signals, the information they hold will be deleted.

- SRAM – This stands for *Static Random Access Memory*. Unlike DRAMs, this kind of memory doesn't require a steady stream of signals. In general, SRAM chips are more complex and expensive than DRAMs. You can use SRAM for cache functions.

- ROM – This is the abbreviation for Read-Only Memory. It is called as such because it prevents the user from editing the memory it contains. Once the data is written on the computer's ROM, it cannot be changed anymore. ROM is usually used to hold the machine's BIOS, since this data is rarely modified.

- CMOS – This is a special type of memory chip. It is designed to hold the configuration settings of a computer's BIOS. CMOS is battery-powered: that means the configuration is retained even if the machine is turned off.

Storage Devices – Their Functions and Characteristics

Computers are useless if they can't store anything. Storage devices hold the information being used, as well as the programs and files the computer needs in order to function properly. In general, storage devices are classified according to their capacity, access time, and physical attributes.

HDD Systems

HDD stands for *Hard Disk Drive*. This storage device is also called hard disk or hard drive. Computers use HDDs to allow quick access to data as well as permanent storage. Typically, hard disks are found inside a computer.

An HDD system is composed of:

Controller – This component controls the storage. It knows how the drive functions, emits signals to the different motors inside the disk, and accepts signals from the sensors within the drive. Nowadays, hard disk manufacturers place the drive and controller in one enclosure.

Hard Disk – This acts as the physical warehouse for the data. HDD systems store data on little disks (about 3-5 inches in diameter) grouped together and kept inside an enclosure.

Host Adapter – This is the system's translator: it converts signals from the controller and hard disk to signals the computer can work with. Most modern motherboards have a built-in host adapter, allowing drive cable connection through board headers.

Floppy Drives

Floppy disks are magnetic storage devices that use plastic diskettes enclosed in a tough casing. Several years ago, floppy disks were used to easily transfer information from one computer to another. Nowadays, few people are using floppy disks because of their small capacity. DVD-ROMs and CD-ROMs have replaced floppy disks in storing and transferring digital information.

CD-ROM Drives

Modern computers use CD-ROM drives. These compact disks are virtually similar to those used in music recording. CD-ROMs allow you to store data for a long period of time. In general, these drives are read-only: you cannot erase or delete the data once it is stored on a CD. In addition, computers need to spend a longer time in "reading" CDs compared to internal hard drives. Why are these drives so popular?

Despite their drawbacks, CD-ROMs are used because they can store large files (about 650MB) and are extremely portable.

DVD-ROM Drives

This is the newest storage device to be used for computers. The DVD (i.e. digital video disc) technology is mostly used for entertainment purposes (e.g. home theater systems). DVD-ROMs are basically similar to the DVDs you use at home. Because of this, computers that are equipped with a DVD-ROM drive can play movies stored on a DVD.

However, DVD-ROMs are way much more useful when used for computers. Since they use newer technology, DVD-ROMs are better than CD-ROMs in terms of storage capacity. On average, DVDs can hold 4GB of data. That means DVD-ROMs are your best option if you are storing or distributing large files.

Important Note: CD-ROMs and DVD-ROMs have the same appearance. The single difference is the logo on the front of DVD drives.

Removable Storage Devices

Many years ago, the term "removable storage" meant something extremely different from what it means now. Tape backup is one of the old storage devices that can still be bought today. Modern computer users prefer the solid-state, random-access removable storage devices. In this section, you'll learn about tape backups and the new storage solutions.

Tape Backup

This is an old type of removable storage. A tape backup device can be installed externally or internally and utilize either an analog or digital magnetic tape to store data. In general, this kind of device can hold more information than other storage mediums. However, they are also one of the slowest in terms of data transfer rate. Because of these reasons, tape backup devices are mainly used for archived information.

Flash Memory

Before, random-access memory chips were only used to access and use data. But now, you'll find them in different physical sizes and storage capacities. Flash memory drives are considered as the best solid-state storage device available. The flash memory category includes SD (secure digital) and other memory cards, USB flash drives, and older detachable and non-detachable memory mechanisms. Each of these storage devices has the capability to store huge amounts of information.

Manufacturers of flash memory devices use revolutionary packaging (e.g. keychain attachments) for their products to provide easy transport options for their end-users.

Chapter 3: How to Work With Computer Parts Effectively

While taking the CompTIA A+ exam, you will answer questions regarding the installation, usage, and replacement of computer parts. This chapter will help you to review regarding those topics.

How to Install, Configure and Optimize Computer Parts

Aside from knowing the characteristics and functions of PC components, you also need to know how to use them. In particular, you should be familiar with the installation, configuration, and optimization of such parts.

How to Upgrade a Storage Device

Storage devices are available in different shapes and sizes. Aside from IDE and SCSI, two of the most popular types, there are SATA (Serial ATA) and PATA (Parallel ATA). You can also differentiate between external and internal drives. This section of the book will explain each of these options.

Preparing the Drive

Regardless of the technology being used, you should format storage devices before using them. Although most drives have their own formatting software, each OS has a tool that you can use. When working with Windows computers, you can utilize the format utility through the command line. If you are working with XP, Vista, 7, or newer Windows system, you can also use the graphical utility program called Disk Management.

How to Work with IDE

Before, IDE (integrated drive electronics) drives were the most popular kind of computer hard drives. Although they are often linked to hard drives, IDE is more than just an interface for hard disks. It can also serve as the interface for different storage types such as Zip, DVD, and CD-ROM.

To install IDE drives, you should:

1. Set the slave/master jumper on the IDE drive.

2. Place the drive inside the drive bay.

3. Connect the cable for power-supply.

4. Link the ribbon cable to the motherboard and to the drive.

5. If the drive isn't detected automatically, you should configure it using the BIOS Setup of your computer.

6. Use your PC's operating system to format and partition the IDE drive.

How to Work with SCSI

SCSI is the abbreviation for *Small Computer System Interface.* This kind of device can be either external or internal to the machine. To configure an SCSI device, you should assign an SCSI ID (also called SCSI address) to all of the devices in the SCSI bus. You can configure their numbers using a jumper or DIP switch.

Whenever the computer sends data to the SCSI device, it emits a signal on the cable assigned to that number. The device will respond with a signal that holds the device's number and the information needed.

You should install a terminator (i.e. terminating resistor device) at the two ends of the bus to keep the SCSI devices working. You can activate and/or deactivate terminators using a jumper.

Here are the things you should do when installing an SCSI device:

- For Internal Devices – Connect the cable (i.e. a 50-wire ribbon cable with multiple keyed connectors) to the adapter and to each SCSI device in your computer. Afterward, place the terminators on the adapter and terminate the final device in the chain. You should leave other devices unterminated.
- For External Devices - Follow the steps outlined above, but here, you should use some stub cables between the SCSI devices in the daisy chain (instead of a long cable that has multiple connectors). Terminate the adapter as well as the final device in the daisy chain (that device should have one stub cable linked to it).
- For Hybrid Devices – Many types of adapters have connectors for external and internal SCSI devices. If you have this kind of adapter, attach the ribbon cable to your internal devices and connect the cable to your adapter. Afterward, daisy-chain the external devices from the external port. Terminate the device at the end of every chain. Make sure that the adapter is unterminated.

External Storage Devices

As capacities shoot up and prices fall down, the number of available external storage devices has increased greatly. Aside from the SCSI variant explained above, you will also see devices with USB connections and those that can connect straight to the system. The computer's operating system will recognize USB devices upon connection. You can just install any additional programs you like to use. A computer program called Dantz Retrospect is included in many storage devices to allow you to utilize external devices as automatic backups.

If the external storage device is linked straight to the system, you can just follow the instructions that came with that product. Then, install additional programs on the computers that you will be using. The main benefit of linking straight to the system is that the storage device/s can be accessed by all of the computers.

How to Upgrade Display Devices

Before linking or unlinking a display device (e.g. a computer monitor), make sure that the computer and the device itself are powered off. Afterward, connect a cable from the computer's video card to the display device. Connect the power cord of that device to an electrical outlet. You may use a modern Digital Visual Interface (DVI) cable or the traditional DB-15 (or VGA) cable.

While installing a new monitor, you should have the proper driver. The driver is the software interface between the display device and the computer's OS. If you don't have the right driver, your monitor won't display what you want to see. Nowadays, you can download the newest drivers from the website of monitor manufacturers.

Aside from the power supply, the most dangerous part to repair is the monitor. Computer technicians say that beginners should never attempt to repair monitors. Monitors can hold high-voltage charges even if they have been powered off for several hours. That means you can be electrocuted if you will try to repair a monitor by yourself. If your monitor stopped working, and you don't want to buy a new one, you should take that device to a TV repair shop or a certified computer technician. The technicians and the repair guys know how to fix monitors properly – they understand the dangers and the correct procedures.

How to upgrade Input and Multimedia Devices

The typical upgrade for input devices is the transition to newer mice and keyboards.

Keyboards

Keyboards may wear out if used repeatedly. The usual problem is "key sticking", where keys are no longer responding to the user. To replace a PS/2 101-key keyboard with a new one, just unplug the old keyboard and plug in the new. As you can see, this is a quick and easy process. Nowadays, however, computer users prefer to replace old keyboards with USB ones.

Here is a principle you need to remember: You can use the "unplug-the-old-and-plug-in-the-new" procedure as long as your computer's OS supports the keyboard you want to use.

Mice

Computer mice also wear out because of repeated use. But don't worry: you can replace old mice with new ones. You may easily replace a PS/2 connection mouse with another without spending too much. As an alternative, you may buy an optical mouse (which prevents dust- and ball-related problems) or a wireless one (which needs batteries to send and receive signals). Although new mouse models still use the PS/2 type of connection, most mouse products in the market use the USB connection.

Chapter 4: The Tools Needed for Checking Computer Parts

The CompTIA A+ exam will also test your skills in checking computer parts. This chapter will help you with that topic by discussing the tools and diagnostic procedures needed.

The Tools Needed by a Computer Technician

A great computer technician needs a great collection of tools. If you are working alone, you may not get past the troubleshooting phase. However, you still need to use certain tools in order to succeed in that task. Once you have identified the problem, you will need to get another set of tools in order to fix it.

This book will focus on the "hardware" tools. These are:

- Screwdrivers – When checking a computer technician's toolkit, you will surely find screwdrivers. Almost all of the big computer parts you'll see today are mounted using screws. If you need to remove these parts, you need to have the right type of screwdriver. This kind of tool is divided into three types:
    - Flat-Blade – Many people refer to this as the *common* or *standard* screwdriver. The screw used with this screwdriver is rarely used today (mainly because the screw's head can be destroyed easily).
    - Phillips – This is perhaps the most popular type of screwdrivers being used today. The screws used with a Phillips screwdriver have enough head surface: you can turn them many times without damaging the screws' head. According to recent reports, more than 90% of the screws used in computers belong to the Phillips-head type.
    - Torx – This is the type of screwdriver you use while working on tiny screws found on Apple and Compaq computers. The screws you remove using a Torx screwdriver have the most surface to work against: they offer the best resistance in terms of screw-head damage. Nowadays, Torx-type screws are gaining more popularity because of their clean and technical look.
- Flashlight – This is one of the tools you should always have. You'll realize how important this tool is when you're crawling under a table searching for a dropped computer part.

- Needle-Nose Pliers – You should have this in your toolkit. This kind of pliers is great for holding connectors or tiny screws (particularly if you have large hands). If needle-nose pliers are still too big to do certain tasks, you may use a pair of tweezers.

- Compressed Air – While working on a computer, you will usually remove the machine's case first. Once the cover is removed, it would be great if you will clean the computer's internal components. The clumps of dirt and fibers can block airflow inside the system unit. As a result, the PC's life will be shortened. The ideal way to eliminate the dust is by using compressed air.

  If you are working for a big company, you probably have a core air compressor that supplies compressed air. If this kind of compressor is not available, you may purchase canned compressed air. However, you'll be shelling out large amounts of money – cans of compressed air are expensive.

- Soldering Iron – You can use it to splice broken wires. Nowadays, computer technicians rarely use this tool. Here's the reason: modern computer parts are created with quick-disconnect connectors. You can easily replace them without splicing anything.

- Wire Strippers – Whenever you have to solder something, you need to use a stripper/wire cutter to prepare the wires for connection. Stripping means you will expose a certain part of the wire by removing the insulation.

- Multi-Meters – This tool is named as such because it is basically a set of different types of testing meters, such as ammeter, voltmeter, and ohmmeter. When used by a trained technician, a multi-meter can identify the failure of various types of computer parts.

  A multi-meter has an analog or digital display, a mode selector switch, and two probes. You can use the switch to perform two things: (1) select the function you want to test and (2) choose the range in which the meter will work. If you need to use an old meter to measure a power pack, you should manually set the range selector. Modern multi-meters, particularly the digital ones, can automatically find the correct ranges.

  Important Note: You should never measure voltage by connecting a manual ranging multi-meter to an AC electrical outlet. This will damage the meter itself, the meter mechanisms, or both.

<u>How to Measure Resistance Using a Multi-Meter</u>

Resistance is the property of electricity commonly measured when troubleshooting computer parts. This electrical property is measured in ohms and represented by the Greek letter "omega." If a multi-meter indicates infinite resistance, the electric currents cannot travel from one prove to another. If you are using a multi-meter to check the resistance and you are getting an infinite reading, there's a huge possibility that the wire is broken.

When measuring resistance, you should set the tool to measure ohms. You can do it using either the selector dial or the front button. Then, connect the PC component you want to measure between the tool's probes. The multi-meter will then show the component's resistance value.

How to Measure Voltage Using a Multi-Meter

This process is similar to the one discussed above, but with two main differences:

1. While measuring voltage, make sure that you properly connect each probe to the source of electricity. For DC voltage, the "-" should be connected to the negative side and the "+" to the positive one. This positioning is irrelevant when measuring AC voltage.

2. You should switch the selector to Volts DC (VDC) or Volts AC (VAC), depending on what you need to measure, to instruct the tool about the voltage you are working with. These settings protect the tool from overload. The multi-meter will blow up if you will plug it into a power source while it's still on "measure resistance" mode.

Chapter 5: Operating Systems

The CompTIA A+ examination will test your knowledge regarding operating systems. Since operating systems play an important role in the computer industry, you should be familiar with them. This chapter will guide you in this topic. Here, you'll learn different things about a computer's OS.

What is an Operating System?

Computers are useless if they don't have any piece of software. Well, you can use them as a doorstop or paperweight – but that is not cost-efficient. You need to have an interface before you can use the capabilities of a computer. And, if you don't know yet, software acts as the interface. Although there are different kinds of software, or computer programs, the most important one you'll ever need is the OS.

Operating systems have various functions, most of which are extremely complex. However, two functions are critical:

1. Interfacing with the computer's hardware

2. Providing an environment in which other pieces of software can run.

Here are the three main types of software that you will encounter in the CompTIA exam:

- Operating System – It provides a stable environment for other computer programs. In addition, it allows the user to enter and execute commands. The operating system gives the user an interface so they can enter commands (i.e. input) and get results or feedback (i.e. output). For this, the OS should communicate with the PC's hardware and conduct the tasks below:

    - Device access
    - Output format
    - Memory management
    - File and disk management

  Once the operating system has performed these basic tasks, the user can enter instructions to the computer using an input device (e.g. a mouse or keyboard). Some of the commands are pre-installed in the operating system, whereas others are given using certain applications. The OS serves as the platform on which the PC's hardware, other pieces of software, and the user work together.

- Application – This is used to complete a specific task. Basically, an application is a computer program written to support the commands given to the OS. Every application is compiled or configured for the operating system it will be used for. Because of this, the application depends on the OS to perform most of its basic functions.

  When a program accesses the computer's memory and linked devices, it sends a request to the OS. The machine's operating system will perform the requests made by the program being used. This setup helps greatly in decreasing the programming overhead, since most of the executable codes are shared – they are written onto the operating system and can be used by different applications installed on the computer.

- Driver – This is an extremely specific program created to instruct an operating system on how to access and use a piece of hardware (e.g. webcam, flash memory, etc.). Every webcam or flash memory has distinct features and settings – the driver helps the OS in knowing how the new hardware works and the things it can do.

The Terms and Concepts Related to Operating Systems

In this section, let's define some of the most important terms and concepts. Study this section carefully since it will teach you the terms you'll encounter during the CompTIA A+ exam.

<u>*Key Terms*</u>

- Source – This is the code that explains how computer programs work. An operating system can be open source or closed source.
  - Open Source – The users have the right to change and examine the code.
  - Closed Source – The users are not allowed to edit or check the code.
- Version – This is a specific variant of a computer program, usually expressed by a number, which informs users regarding the "newness" of the software. For instance, MS-DOS is now in its sixth main version. Computer programmers distinguish minor revisions from major ones this way:
  - "Program" 4.0 to "Program" 5.0 is a major revision.
  - "Program" 5.0 to "Program" 5.2 is a minor revision.

- Shell – A piece of software that works on top of the operating system. It allows users to execute commands through an array of menus or a different type of graphical interface. A shell makes an operating system simpler and easier to use by modifying the GUI (graphical user interface).
- GUI – The method by which a user communicates with computers. A GUI uses a touchpad, mouse, or a different mechanism (aside from a keyboard) to interact with the machine and issue commands.
- Multithreading – The capability of a computer program to contain several requests in the computer's CPU. Since it allows an application to perform different tasks simultaneously, computers experience a boost in performance and efficiency.
- Network – A group of computers that are connected by a communication link. A network allows computers to share resources and information.
- Preemptive Multitasking – This is a multitasking technique in which the operating system allocates each program a certain amount of CPU time. Afterward, the OS takes back the control and provides another task or program access to the CPU. Basically, if a computer program crashes, the operating system takes the processor from the faulty program and gives it to the next one (which must be working). Even though unstable computer programs still get locked, only the affected application will stop – not the whole machine.
- Cooperative Multitasking – This is a multitasking technique that relies on the applications themselves. Here, each program is responsible for utilizing and giving up access to the CPU. Windows 3.1 used this method to manage multiple programs. If an application stalls while it is using the CPU, the application fails to free the CPU properly, and the whole computer gets locked, the user needs to reboot the machine.

Conclusion

Thank you again for purchasing this book!

I hope this book was able to help you to prepare for the CompTIA A+ tests.

The next step is to reread this book and use other information sources. That way, you can increase your chances of passing the exam.

Finally, if you enjoyed this book, please take the time to share your thoughts and post a review on Amazon. It'd be greatly appreciated!

Thank you and good luck!

www.ingramcontent.com/pod-product-compliance
Lightning Source LLC
Chambersburg PA
CBHW061040050326
40689CB00012B/2910
9781523662524